RABBITS

by Herbert S. Zim

pictures by Joy Buba

WILLIAM MORROW AND COMPANY:

NEW YORK, 1948

Thanks are due to Dr. Frank G. Ashbrook,
U. S. Fish and Wildlife Service,
for reading and criticizing the manuscript.

18 19 20

For Winnie, Roger and Thumper, the Rabbit

Seven great continents make up our earth and rabbits live on six of them. No rabbits live in the cold Antarctic, but neither do any other land animals. Most people know rabbits because there is hardly a country without them. You can surely see wild rabbits, since they live in every State: in marshes, meadows, mountains, and the vast plains.

There are many more wild rabbits than tame ones, and many kinds of wild rabbits. Rabbits are close relatives of rats and mice. They have the same kind of sharp, gnawing teeth. But anyone who has seen a mouse scamper across the

RABBIT **RAT**

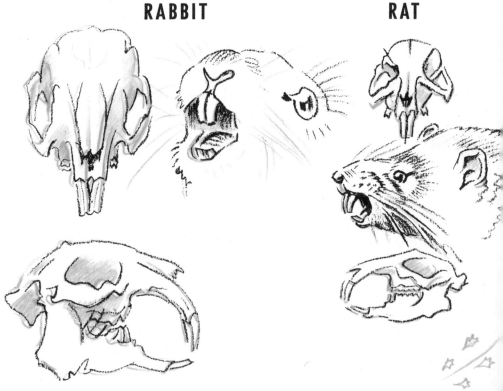

MOUSE TRACKS

SITTING

floor and a cottontail hop into the briars knows how rabbits and mice differ. Mice and rats are the most common animals in the world. Next come the rabbits and hares.

RABBIT TRACKS

Hares are a larger and slightly different kind of rabbit. A hare's ears and legs are longer. But some rabbits are called hares and some hares are called rabbits. That mixes things up. One hare is the snowshoe rabbit, so named because its large furry feet act like snowshoes on the soft snow. Jack rabbits are

SNOWSHOE

JACK

COTTONTAIL

western hares that live mostly on the dry prairies. They can outrun a dog and can leap as much as twenty feet.

9

SPY HOP

SLOW WALK-HOP

The snowshoe rabbits are white in winter and brown in summer. The jack rabbits are usually brown. One kind has a black tail; another kind has white. They all build a nest or form in the grass and brush. The form is

SUMMER   AUTUMN

a hollow where the grass has been
smoothed down so that the hares can
rest and hide. Their fur matches the
ground or the snow so well that a hunter
can pass just a few feet away and not see
a jack rabbit or snowshoe rabbit lying
quietly near him.

Cottontail rabbits are smaller wild rabbits that often visit our gardens. They scamper away when you come near, their white tails flashing behind. This white tail is easy to see when the cottontail is running. It is white only on the underside and cannot be seen unless the cottontail is in motion.

We see the cottontails often because they do not like the deep woods but live along the edges of fields and meadows. Here they find plenty to eat close to the briars and tangles where they can hide from their enemies. Like the hares, cottontails make forms where they lie hiding. They also burrow under the snow or in the ground and sometimes hide in hollow logs or under rocks. Brush rabbits, pygmy rabbits, and swamp rabbits are very much like the cottontails, but they do not have the white tail patch.

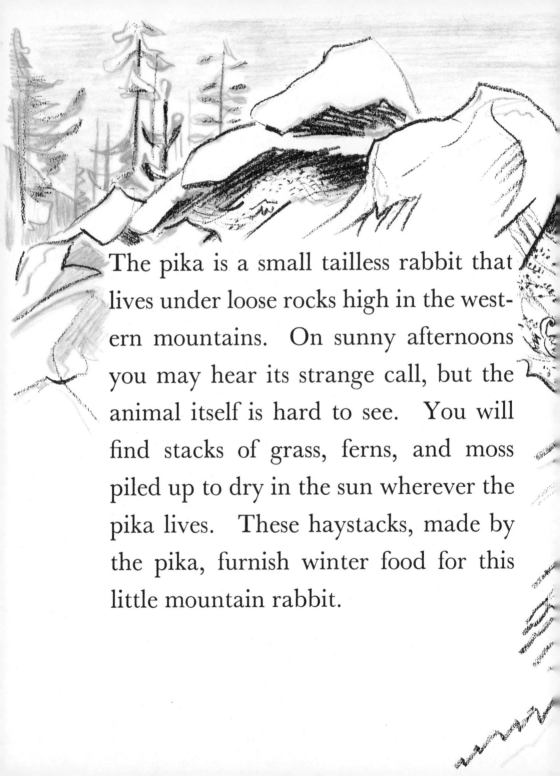

The pika is a small tailless rabbit that lives under loose rocks high in the western mountains. On sunny afternoons you may hear its strange call, but the animal itself is hard to see. You will find stacks of grass, ferns, and moss piled up to dry in the sun wherever the pika lives. These haystacks, made by the pika, furnish winter food for this little mountain rabbit.

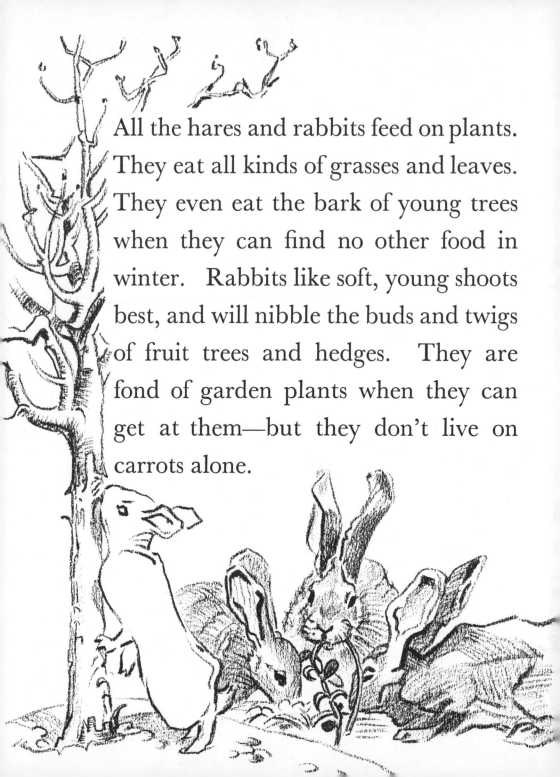

All the hares and rabbits feed on plants.
They eat all kinds of grasses and leaves.
They even eat the bark of young trees
when they can find no other food in
winter. Rabbits like soft, young shoots
best, and will nibble the buds and twigs
of fruit trees and hedges. They are
fond of garden plants when they can
get at them—but they don't live on
carrots alone.

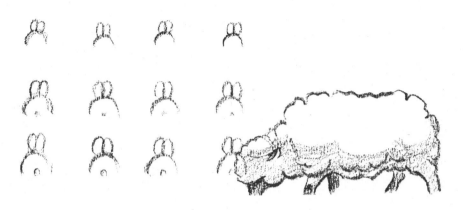

Rabbits are active animals. They eat
a lot. Twelve jack rabbits eat as much
of the thin prairie grass as one sheep,
and sixty rabbits eat as much as a cow.

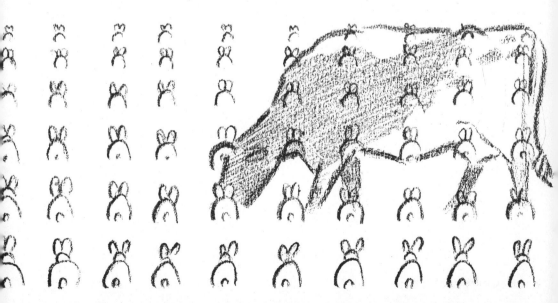

There are thousands and thousands of jack rabbits. Farmers don't like them at all. Farmers don't like the cottontails either, for during the winter, hungry cottontails may kill a whole orchard of young apple trees by eating the bark. The farmers build fences through which rabbits cannot crawl, and under which they cannot dig. In Australia a fence nine hundred miles long keeps millions of rabbits out of the sheep land. Wire guards are put around young trees, and farmers spray them with chemicals that rabbits do not like. Some farmers set traps for rabbits. They hunt and kill many, many rabbits each year, but there always seem to be more.

Rabbits and hares are hunted for other reasons, too. People like rabbit meat. So millions of wild and tame rabbits find their way to the butcher's each year. Rabbit fur is very useful. Men's and women's felt hats are made of rabbit fur. A furrier can take rabbit skins and change the fur until it no longer looks or feels like rabbit. Coats made of rabbit skins were once sold under such names as Belgian beaver, French sable, and Baltic black fox.

But even without hunters, trappers, and farmers, rabbits do not have an easy time. They have always had natural enemies waiting to seize and eat them.

Hawks and owls swoop down from the sky. Foxes, weasels, coyotes, and wild-cats come prowling from the woods. Black snakes glide through the grass. All of these eat rabbits when they can catch them. The rabbits have only two ways to protect themselves. They can avoid danger if they can keep from being seen. Rabbits may freeze and remain perfectly still when danger is near. Once seen, the rabbit's only chance is to run and dodge to get into briars, rocks, or some hole till his enemy goes away. In spite of all these enemies we still have many hares and rabbits. Hares and rabbits have a great many young. So though many are killed, many more remain. Three or four young are born in every litter and each year the mother has several litters. A mother cottontail may raise a dozen young a year. She builds a nest, using

grass, and fur from her body. After her young are born, blind and naked, she cares for them. The mother rabbit is easily frightened. If someone disturbs her nest, she may run away and not return to her young any more.

The babies' eyes open soon and their fur begins to grow. In about two months they begin to eat grass and take care of themselves.

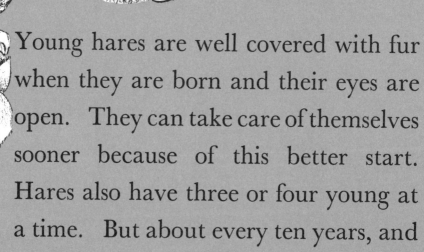

HARE

RABBIT

Young hares are well covered with fur when they are born and their eyes are open. They can take care of themselves sooner because of this better start. Hares also have three or four young at a time. But about every ten years, and

we don't know why, many snowshoe
hares have up to eight or ten young to
a litter.   Then the number of hares in-
creases rapidly, and they overrun the
northern woods.   The wildcats, foxes,
and all animals that feed on the hares
grow fat because they have more food.

27

Then, almost suddenly, the hares begin to die off, perhaps from a disease. The number of hares becomes very low and stays low for some time, till a new increase begins.

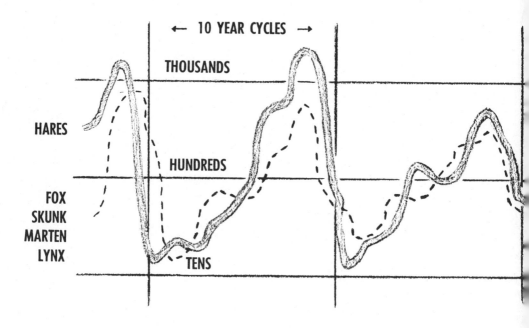

For about two thousand years people
have tamed rabbits for pets and raised
them for food.   Poor people, who could
not afford a cow or goat, raised rabbits
for meat.   Rabbit raising became more
and more important.   Some people

earn their living raising rabbits. Now the United States Government has a large laboratory in California where scientists study better ways of raising rabbits and keeping them healthy.

For a long time tamed rabbits looked very much like wild ones. Then, by accident and through breeding, different kinds of rabbits began to appear. Rabbit breeders tried to produce rabbits with more meat and heavier fur. Soon there were various breeds of rabbits, each a bit different from the others. Among all animals every now and then some are born with white fur and pink

eyes. These are called albinos. We have albino mice, cats, foxes, guinea pigs, and rabbits.

The albino rabbits, pure white in color, have become favorite pets.

Many breeds of rabbits we raise came from Europe and have been in our country for less than a century. The Belgian hare, really a rabbit, was one of the first brought here. It is still well-known, though it is no longer a common breed. New Zealand rabbits have been developed from the Belgian hare. The com-

mon white rabbit is likely to be a New
Zealand White. Then there is the
Flemish Giant, bred for its fur and
meat; the French Silver, a medium-
sized rabbit; the Chinchilla rabbit
with its thick, beautiful fur; and the
Himalayan, a white rabbit with black
nose, ears, and feet.

The Himalayan and the New Zealand White make fine pets.

BELGIAN

NEW ZEALAND
(WHITE)

FLEMISH GIANT

FRENCH SILVER

HIMALAYAN

ANGORA

CHINCHILLA

The Angora rabbit is something special. It's not a large rabbit, but it grows a heavy crop of long, soft wool. One Angora rabbit grows as much as a pound of wool a year—and a pound of this light, fluffy wool is worth quite a sum. The rabbits are plucked or sheared four or five times a year with special electric clippers. The white, tan, or blackish wool is used to make sweaters, mittens, scarves, and coats.

Some breeds of rabbits are valuable. Some are very odd, like the lop-eared rabbit with ears over two feet long. But the kind you are likely to buy or get as a pet will be one of the breeds just mentioned. Rabbits make good pets though they cannot be trained like a dog. They will come to you and eat from your hand. They are quiet, gentle, and easy to care for and raise.

Getting a rabbit is just the beginning. You must learn to handle, feed, and house it. The real fun comes in raising a healthy, happy pet. Perhaps later you may want to breed rabbits of your own. None of these things is hard to do, but a rabbit needs care if you want to raise it properly.

Most rabbits sold or given as pets are young ones that need more care than older rabbits. They must be handled carefully. Ears are not handles. Never use them to pick a rabbit up. Lift a

rabbit as the pictures show.   Rabbits

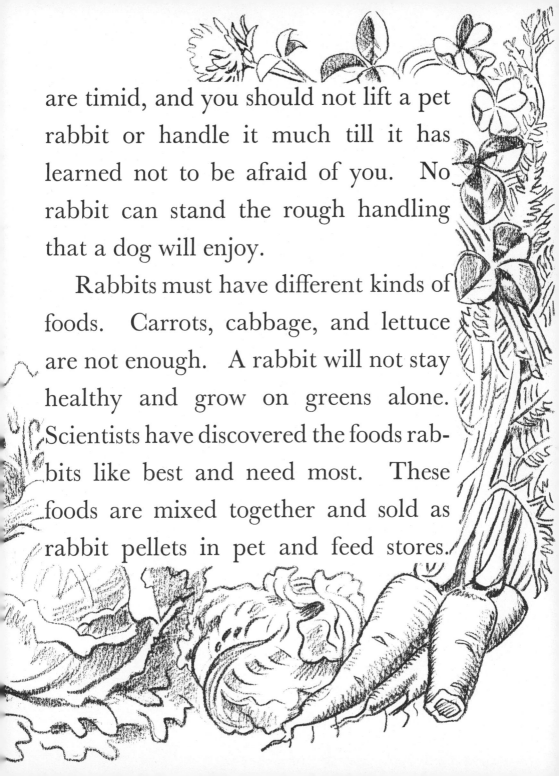

are timid, and you should not lift a pet rabbit or handle it much till it has learned not to be afraid of you. No rabbit can stand the rough handling that a dog will enjoy.

Rabbits must have different kinds of foods. Carrots, cabbage, and lettuce are not enough. A rabbit will not stay healthy and grow on greens alone. Scientists have discovered the foods rabbits like best and need most. These foods are mixed together and sold as rabbit pellets in pet and feed stores.

This kind of rabbit food contains every-thing the rabbit needs. The rabbit will enjoy any vegetables or even lawn grass. But these are extras and should not take place of the pellets.

If you cannot get pellets, feed the rabbit grains, such as oats, wheat, or buckwheat. Corn is not as good. Mix soybeans or peanuts with the grains if you have them. Then give the rabbit chopped clover or alfalfa hay, some greens, and a salt spool to lick. Add a bit of dry bread now and then. A rab-bit needs all these foods to keep healthy and grow.

SALT

It is not true that rabbits can live without water. Wild rabbits get water from dew-covered grass. Tame rabbits should have water in a heavy dish they cannot turn over. The dish must be kept clean and the water changed every day. In warm weather a large rabbit will drink about a pint of water daily.

How a rabbit is fed may be just as important as what it is fed. Food that is dumped on the floor of the cage to get wet and spoil may do the rabbit harm. Rabbits are more active at night than during the day, so it is better to feed them in the evening. Build a bin for

the hay and put pellets in a heavy dish.
Then the rabbit can help itself without
wasting food and spoiling it.   Give the
rabbit carrot tops and trimmings from
vegetables, but nothing spoiled.   If the
rabbit has not eaten the fresh food over-
night, remove it in the morning.

A rabbit house is called a hutch. A hutch is a home for one rabbit or for a mother rabbit and her young. After the young are grown, each needs a hutch of its own. Hutches are usually built two feet high, two feet wide, and four to six feet long. The larger size is better for raising a family of rabbits. A

number of hutches can be set up in a row, or even built one on top of the other. The best kind of hutch is built with walls and floor of heavy wire screen. Such a hutch is easy to keep clean and so is healthier for the rabbit.

Wooden floors become damp and are hard to clean. A good hutch can be made of a wood frame covered with wire screen. For each hutch you will need a water crock and a food rack. Sometimes people get a rabbit before they have a hutch and must find a place to put it. Any large wooden box will do—the larger the better. Put two inches of sawdust, wood shavings, or torn newspaper on the bottom. Cover the box with a heavy wire screen. Such a cage is only temporary, and if it is not cleaned every day it will quickly become wet and smelly.

Hutches can be kept outdoors, but they should be protected from rain and wind, so some type of shelter is needed.   This

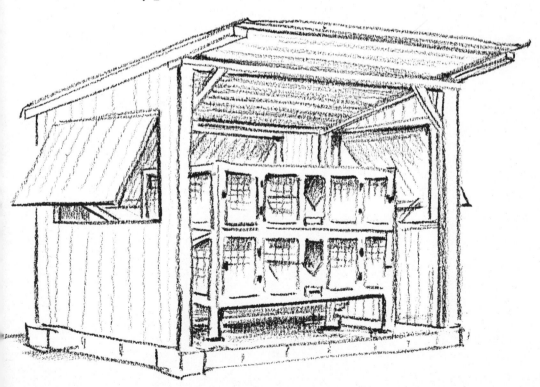

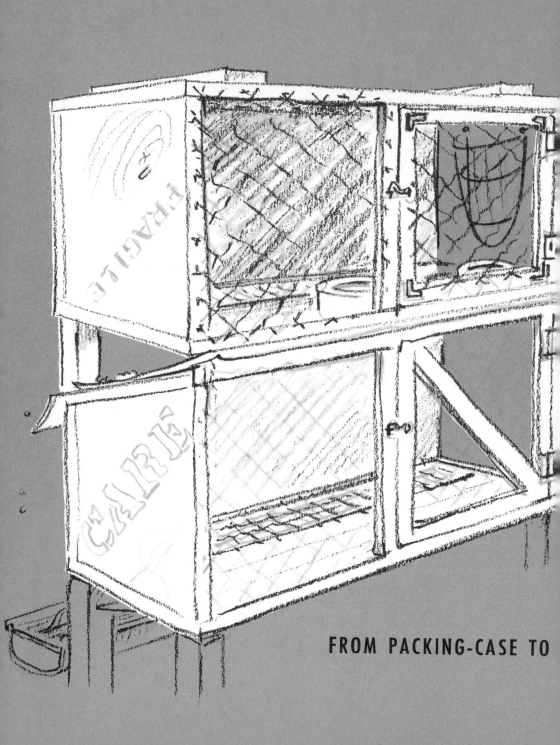

FROM PACKING-CASE TO

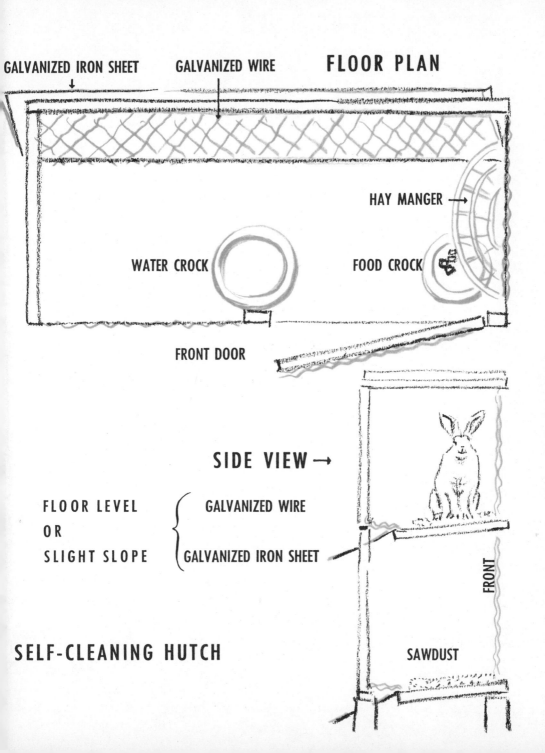

FLOOR PLAN

GALVANIZED IRON SHEET GALVANIZED WIRE

HAY MANGER →

WATER CROCK FOOD CROCK

FRONT DOOR

SIDE VIEW →

FLOOR LEVEL
OR
SLIGHT SLOPE
{ GALVANIZED WIRE

GALVANIZED IRON SHEET

FRONT

SELF-CLEANING HUTCH

SAWDUST

may be a simple shed or a part of a garage or barn. Rabbits will stay healthy if they have this protection, if the hutch is kept clean, and if they are given the proper food and water.

If their cages are wet and smelly or if their food is spoiled, rabbits get sick. A sick rabbit should be removed from the others since some rabbit diseases are

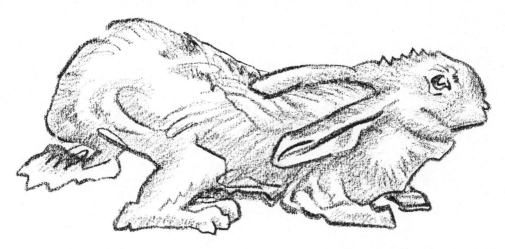

catching. Keep a sharp lookout for sneezing, running nose, scabby ears, sore feet, and matted-down fur. These are signs of poor health.

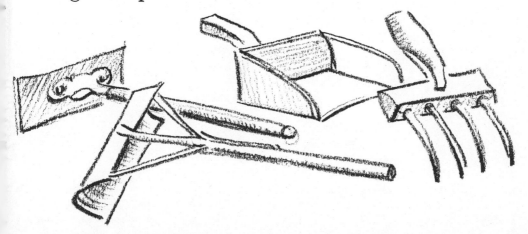

You really begin to know rabbits when you start to raise them. Think carefully and get good advice before you begin. The babies are exciting to watch, but what will you do with them after they are grown? To raise a rabbit family, you will need a male and a female rabbit—both over six months old. The male rabbit is called a buck. The female is called a doe. They should be kept in separate hutches. When you

want to start raising your rabbits, put the doe in the buck's hutch for a few hours. Then return the doe to her own hutch. Thirty days later, the mother rabbit should have her young.

The mother rabbit will want a nest where her young can be born. Help her by making a nesting box out of an old nail keg, laid on its side, with a board nailed across half the front. Fill the

bottom with hay. A few days before
the young are born, the mother will
start to make a nest in the nesting box.
She will pull fur from her own body and
mix it with the hay. She may be rest-
less, so don't bother her. The young

are likely to be born at night, and the mother may remain in the nest box with them.   Do not disturb her in any way. Leave food and water for her, but don't clean and fuss around.   If the mother is frightened, she may not feed her litter or she may injure them.

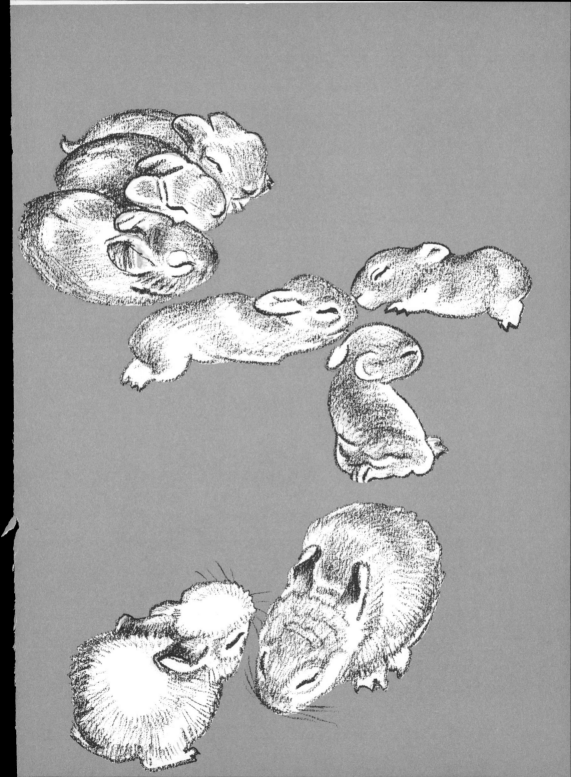

After a few days, you can look at the small naked rabbits, as small as your little finger. There may be from four to ten of them, since tame rabbits often have larger litters than the wild ones. People who raise rabbits usually kill the weakest of the young if there are more than six in a litter. The mother rabbit cannot feed or give her young proper care if there are more than six. The re-

maining young will grow better if the extra ones are killed. The young grow fast. Their eyes begin to open in ten days and their fur begins to grow. In about three weeks they can nibble on soft vegetables, though they still nurse from their mother, too. When the young are about two months old they leave their mother entirely. Then they are big enough to be put in a large hutch

where they can live together. In another two months, each will need a hutch of its own. When you reach this stage you no longer have pet rabbits. You're in the rabbit business now!

NO RENEWALS!

**PLEASE RETURN BOOK AND REQUEST
AGAIN.**